INSIDE SPECIAL FORCES ™

SPECIAL OPS:
AIR COMMANDOS

Jeri Freedman

rosen publishing's
rosen central

New York

Published in 2015 by The Rosen Publishing Group, Inc.
29 East 21st Street, New York, NY 10010

First Edition

Library of Congress Cataloging-in-Publication Data

Freedman, Jeri.
Special ops: Air Commandos/Jeri Freedman.—1st edition.
        pages cm.—(Inside special ops)
Includes bibliographical references and index.
ISBN 978-1-4777-7993-4 (library bound)—ISBN 978-1-4777-7994-1
(pbk.)—ISBN 978-1-4777-7995-8 (6-pack)
1. United States. Air Force—Commando troops—Juvenile literature.
2. United States. Air Force Special Operations Command—Juvenile
literature. 3. Special operations (Military science)—Juvenile literature.
4. Special forces (Military science)—United States—Juvenile literature.
I. Title.
UG633.F72 2014
358.4—dc23

2014012601

Manufactured in Malaysia

CONTENTS

INTRODUCTION

Counterterrorism actions, efforts to combat drug lords, and clandestine military operations around the world have sparked an interest in the elite Special Forces of the U.S. military. Special Forces engage in unconventional combat operations. They are an elite fighting force subject to a rigorous selection and training process. They perform highly dangerous and often secret operations.

The history of U.S. Special Forces dates back to the formation of the United States. As far back as the Revolutionary War (1775–1783), colonial soldier Francis Marion engaged in guerrilla, or unconventional, warfare. Leading a group of irregular militiamen over swampy territory, Marion was extraordinarily successful at striking at the British swiftly and withdrawing quickly. His attacks and intelligence gathering were so effective that the frustrated British dubbed him "the swamp fox." Marion would go on to form an elite group of soldiers that was one of the earliest examples of Army Rangers.

Modern Special Forces have their roots in units formed during World War II (1939–1945). Early units involved in special operations included the 6th Army Special Reconnaissance Unit, known as the Alamo Scouts. This unit operated in the Pacific Theater, the area of war between the Allied forces and Japan. It is renowned for operations such as the freeing of

By parachuting into otherwise inaccessible areas, special operations soldiers are able to gain access to targets that are impossible for regular troops to reach.

prisoners of war (POWs) from the Japanese POW camp at Cabanatuan in the Philippines in 1945. The direct predecessor to today's Special Forces command was the Office of Special Services, which recruited members of the armed forces for secret missions during World War II.

Airborne units, such as the 82nd Airborne, have their roots in World War II as well. Airborne soldiers, known as paratroopers, played a key role in many major battles, including the invasion of Normandy. Parachuting soldiers are able to achieve access to sites that are inaccessible from the ground. Today, air commandos are involved in special military operations, counterinsurgency, and counterterrorism. In addition, they are called upon to intervene in grave emergencies and natural disasters. This resource examines the role that air commandos play in these operations. It covers their dramatic history, their selection and training regimen, and some of their most exciting missions.

AIRBORNE SPECIAL OPERATIONS

Airborne Special Forces parachute into remote and dangerous locales to carry out missions. Airborne missions require two types of soldiers—paratroopers, who parachute into these regions, and the pilots and crew who fly the aircraft that deliver the paratroopers to their destination and provide air support for them. This material explains the nature of airborne special operations and the various units that are involved in them.

WHAT ARE AIRBORNE SPECIAL OPERATIONS?

Airborne Special Forces are helicopter units. The missions of airborne units involve reconnaissance, attack, and assault actions. Reconnaissance missions involve the use of aircraft and airborne personnel to discover information about the enemy, such as the distribution of troops and troop movements. In assault missions, specially trained light infantry forces parachute into a war zone and use portable and lightweight weapons to carry out attacks on enemy forces. In attack missions, aircraft of the airborne units use missiles, bombs, and other weapons to attack enemy positions.

WHO ARE THE AIRBORNE SPECIAL OPERATIONS GROUPS?

The airborne special operations units are overseen by the United States Army Special Operations Command (Airborne) (USASOC). The command's mission is to organize U.S. Army Special Forces. USASOC selects and trains Special Forces recruits, then deploys Special Forces units and conducts missions worldwide. USASOC maintains a number of different types of Special Forces units, as well as support groups responsible for equipping, supplying, and supporting Special Forces. Its headquarters is at Fort Bragg, North Carolina.

USASOC is responsible for missions that involve unconventional warfare, foreign internal defense, reconnaissance, and counterterrorism (fighting terrorists). Unconventional warfare consists of military operations in situations where it is not feasible to use regular military troops. Foreign internal defense operations employ the Special Forces to work with the police and military forces of friendly developing nations to improve their skills. They also help with humanitarian and disaster relief projects. At times they engage in search and rescue missions, and in peacekeeping and security activities.

Airborne Special Forces also engage in coalition warfare, which requires them to work jointly with the forces of other countries. USASOC oversees many types of Special Forces divisions. Here the focus is on the 75th Rangers Regiment (Airborne) and the 160th Special Operations Aviation Regiment (SOAR), as well as on other army divisions that are often involved in airborne special operations today.

U.S. soldiers, including Special Forces servicemen, collect gear from a Chinook helicopter in Afghanistan. Airborne Special Forces soldiers are often deployed in short-term, intense operations.

75TH RANGER REGIMENT (AIRBORNE)

The 75th Ranger Regiment is a light infantry special operations force. It is an agile, flexible force and functions as the army's premier raid force. It deploys more often than conventional army units, but for shorter-duration, more intense operations. It has the capability for both air assault and light action raids. Direct action raids are short-duration strikes and small-scale offensive actions that use specialized military capabilities to seize or destroy targets. The goal of such a raid may also be to capture, recover, or damage designated targets. Rangers can be employed in squads of a dozen men or less, or in very large units. Today the Rangers tend to perform small unit operations, similar to those traditionally carried out by special operations units such as the Delta Force and Navy SEALs.

The history of the Rangers dates back to the mid-1700s, when Captain Benjamin Church and Major Robert Rogers formed Ranger units during King Philip's War (1675–1678) and the French and Indian War (1754–1763). During the Revolutionary War, the Continental Congress formed eight companies of expert riflemen, which were dubbed the Corps of Rangers. At the same time, Francis Marion organized a separate group of solders, which became famous as a ranger unit.

During the War of 1812 (1812–1815), Rangers patrolled the frontier from Ohio to western Illinois. Daniel Boone and Abraham Lincoln were among those

Rangers. During the Civil War (1861–1865), John Singleton Mosby became renowned as a Confederate Ranger for his raids on the Union army. However, after the Civil War, the use of Ranger units lapsed until World War II, when Major (later Brigadier General) William O. Darby organized the first modern Ranger unit, the 1st Ranger Battalion. He modeled the Rangers on the British commandos. Darby's Rangers played an important role in some of the best-known battles of World War II, including the D-Day landings at Normandy, France. The 75th Infantry Regiment was first organized during World War II, in the Pacific, where

This 1967 photo shows an airborne Special Forces team in flight in a South Vietnam war zone during the Vietnam War. Airborne special operations were often necessary to reach jungle targets.

the United States was battling the Japanese. Its commander was Major General Frank D. Merrill, and it was dubbed Merrill's Marauders.

The Ranger battalions were deactivated at the close of WWII but reactivated during the Korean War (1950–1953). Fifteen Ranger companies participated in the Korean War beginning in 1950. Their activities included scouting, ambushes, assaults, and regaining lost positions through counterattacks. Thirteen Ranger units served in Vietnam during the Vietnam War (1954–1975), and the Rangers participated extensively in the wars in Iraq and Iran. Most recently, they have been involved in counterterrorism activities.

160TH SPECIAL OPERATIONS AVIATION REGIMENT (AIRBORNE)

Control of the combat aspects of Special Forces aviation is provided by the U.S. Army Special Operations Aviation Command (ARSOAC) division of USASOC. Operating under the command and control of the Special Aviation Command is the 160th Special Operations Aviation Regiment (SOAR), which trains and deploys army special operations aviation forces around the world. They are called "the Night Stalkers" because they are experts at attacking under cover of darkness without being detected. They fly specially modified Chinook and Black Hawk helicopters as well as attack configurations of Little Bird helicopters.

The 160th SOAR(A) was originally created as Task Force 160 in 1981 at Fort Campbell, Kentucky. It was formed from soldiers of the 101st Airborne and designated the 160th Aviation Battalion. It officially became an airborne unit in 1986 and was called the 160th Special Operations Aviation Group (Airborne). It was designated the Special Operations Aviation Regiment in 1990.

The 160th SOAR(A) consists of a regimental headquarters, four battalions, and a dedicated training company. The regiment headquarters, 1st and 2nd Battalions, and Special Operations Aviation Training Battalion are located at Fort Campbell, Kentucky. The 3rd Battalion is based at Hunter Army Airfield, Georgia, and the 4th Battalion is based at Fort Lewis, Washington.

82ND AIRBORNE

The 82nd Airborne Division is an active duty airborne infantry division that specializes in parachute assault operations. The 82nd Airborne has a long and impressive history. It has its roots in the 82nd Infantry Division, which was formed in 1917 at Camp Gordon, Georgia. The United States at that time consisted of forty-eight states, and the division's members came from all forty-eight. Therefore, the 82nd was dubbed the "All-Americans." The 82nd fought major campaigns in World War I but was disbanded at the end of the war. Twenty years later, in 1942, the 82nd was activated once again, this time

THE NIGHT STALKER CREED

The 160th Special Operations Aviation Regiment is also known as the Night Stalkers because of its expertise in nighttime operations. The following is the creed of the Night Stalkers:

Service in the 160th is a calling only a few will answer, for the mission is constantly demanding and hard. And when the impossible has been accomplished, the only reward is another mission that no one else will try. As a member of the Night Stalkers, I am a tested volunteer, seeking only to safeguard the honor and prestige of my country, by serving the elite Special Operations Soldiers of the United States. I pledge to maintain my body, mind and equipment in a constant state of readiness for I am a member of the fastest deployable Task Force in the world—ready to move at a moment's notice anytime, anywhere, arriving on target plus or minus 30 seconds.

I guard my unit's mission with secrecy, for my only true ally is the night and the element of surprise. My manner is that of the Special Operations Quiet Professional, secrecy is a way of life. In battle, I eagerly meet the enemy for I volunteered to be up front where the fighting is hard. I fear no foe's ability, nor underestimate his will to fight.

The mission and my precious cargo are my concern. I will never surrender. I will never leave a fallen comrade to fall into the hands of the enemy and under no circumstances will I ever embarrass my country.

Gallantly will I show the world and the elite forces I support that a Night Stalker is a specially selected and well trained soldier.

I serve with the memory and pride of those who have gone before me for they loved to fight, fought to win and would rather die than quit.

Night Stalkers Don't Quit!

under the command of Major General Omar N. Bradley. That year, the 82nd became the first airborne division in the U.S. Army.

The division played a role in major battles of World War II, including parachute assaults into Sicily and Salerno, Italy. It also engaged in the most significant airborne operation of the war— the airborne invasion of Normandy, code-named Operation Neptune. The invasion was the largest airborne assault in history, and the 82nd Airborne used hundreds of planes and gliders to deliver parachute and glider infantry to Normandy, France. After the war, the 82nd Airborne returned to Fort Bragg, North Carolina. Since that time, it has been involved in military operations, counter-terrorism, and counterinsurgency (responding to dangerous uprisings) around the world.

101ST AIRBORNE (AIR ASSAULT) DIVISION

The 101st Airborne Division has been frequently involved in major counterinsurgency, counterter-rorism, and other special operations missions. The 101st Airborne Division is a U.S. Army light infantry division specially trained for air assault operations

Paratroopers of the 82nd Airborne parachute into Fort Bragg, North Carolina, where the division is stationed. Parachuting skills are an important part of the training at Fort Bragg.

using airplanes. Its nickname is "the Screaming Eagles." The division was activated August 16, 1942, at Camp Claiborne, Louisiana. In the 1940s, it became famous for its role in World War II, which included the D-Day landings at Normandy, France; Operation Market Garden, the liberation of the Netherlands; and the Battle of the Bulge, which took place around the city of Bastogne, Belgium.

In the Vietnam War, the 101st Airborne Division participated in a number of major operations, among them the battle for Hamburger Hill in May 1969. It switched from flying airplanes to helicopters, and in 1969 it was reorganized as an airmobile division and then as an air assault division in 1974. The division is headquartered at Fort Campbell, Kentucky. In 2008, the 101st Airborne was part of Combined Joint Task Force 101 in Operation Enduring Freedom in Afghanistan. The force operated in an area that covered fourteen provinces and included much of the border area between Afghanistan and Pakistan and the Hindu Kush and Afghan Controlled Highlands. It supported the new Afghan government and implemented 2,500 development projects. The division trained the Afghan National Security Forces and with them rooted out insurgents. The division was part of the operation in which Special Forces soldiers and Navy SEALs killed Osama bin Laden, founder of Al Qaeda. They are still active in Afghanistan and Iraq as part of U.S. counterterrorism operations.

CHAPTER 2

SELECTION, TRAINING, AND PREPARATION

All Special Forces personnel volunteer to be part of the elite group. (At this time, women are not eligible to be a part of the Special Forces.) Qualifying for special operations is difficult, requiring superior mental as well as physical skills. The process of selection and training of Special Forces is designed to identify which soldiers have the capabilities that will make them successful under the demanding conditions they will face in the Special Forces.

RANGER TRAINING

Ranger training takes place at Fort Benning, Georgia. Ranger training focuses on five major areas: small unit tactics, mobility, marksmanship, physical training, and medical training. Rangers must endure very dangerous and difficult missions, and their training is designed to expose their minds and bodies to conditions as close as possible to the extremely stressful conditions they will experience in the field, where they must make rapid decisions in dangerous situations. Ranger training takes place over two months in three phases: Crawl, Walk, and Run.

The Crawl Phase is designed to evaluate whether the soldiers volunteering have the required physical and mental skills to complete the training successfully. The Crawl Phase lasts twenty days. In the first days, applicants are evaluated. The Ranger Physical Fitness Test (RPFT) is administered, and soldiers must be able to accomplish the following:

- Push-ups: 49 (in two minutes, graded strictly for perfect form)
- Sit-ups: 59 (in two minutes)
- Chin-ups: 6 (performed from a dead hang with no lower body movement)

They must also complete a 5-mile (8-kilometer) run in forty minutes or less and complete the Combat Water Survival Assessment, which requires the student to walk across a log suspended 35 feet (11 meters) above a pond, then move on to a rope crawl, then jump into the water and shed his rifle and equipment while submerged, before climbing a 70-foot (21 m) ladder and descending back into the pond on a pulley on a suspended cable. Failure to complete any of these tasks will result in the student being dropped from the school. Students land navigation test. Other challenges include completing a demanding obstacle course, demolitions training, and a 12-mile (19 km) forced march with full gear that must be completed within three hours. According to the Airborne and Ranger Training Brigade website, 60 percent of applicants who drop out of Ranger School do so in the first four days.

The Walk Phase takes place in the mountains at Camp Merrill, near Dahlonega, Georgia, over twenty-one days. Students learn mountaineering skills as well as how to sustain themselves in the mountains. They

also continue combat training. Students are required to execute combat missions that require mountaineering skills. Missions require parachuting into small drop zones, air assaults into the mountains, moving cross country over mountains, vehicle ambushes, raiding communications and mortar sites, river crossings, and scaling steep mountain terrain. Upon completing the Walk Phase, students embark on an airborne "mission," parachuting into Camp James E. Rudder at Eglin Air Force Base, Florida, for the final phase of training.

The Run Phase training furthers the students' ability to lead small units on airborne and air assault missions. It also covers missions involving small-boat, ship-to-shore, and on-foot combat patrol operations. Students learn to operate in swamp and rain forest environments. Students are assessed on their ability to accomplish raids, ambushes, and urban assaults. Because of the increased emphasis on dealing with terrorists, counterinsurgency, and war in an urban environment, there are many scenarios that take place in urban environments, missions using combat outposts, convoy operations with improvised explosive devices (IEDs), and actions dealing with various types of opposing forces who are reluctant fighters, die-hard insurgents, or martyrs such as suicide bombers. Training is also given in emergency medical evacuation procedures such as medical and casualty evacuation (MEDEVAC/CASEVAC) operations.

Only about 50 percent of those who attend Ranger School graduate. Those who successfully

SPECIAL OPERATIONS COMMAND PARACHUTE TEAM

The U.S. Special Operations Command has an exhibition parachute team, which performs aerial parachute stunts. The team, formed in 1991, seeks to create interest in parachuting in the Special Forces for recruitment purposes.

Members of the parachute team are all volunteers from the Special Forces. Team members are highly skilled and experienced in a variety of combatant and humanitarian missions. They use skills that in the field are part of clandestine insertion during missions. Among the techniques is the dangerous and difficult military free fall. Members perform with the team in addition to carrying out their regular duties. They are chosen after a rigorous training program, and training for performances is conducted during members' off-duty hours.

The team performs intricate maneuvers and precision canopy control techniques, including carrying a U.S. flag or passing a baton. They wear burning smoke canisters attached to their boots so that the audience can see them more clearly. Jumping from an aircraft flying at 12,500 feet (3,800 m) and free-falling about 2 miles (3.2 km) before opening their parachutes, they reach speeds greater than 120 miles per hour (193 kilometers per hour). During free fall, the members of the team create numerous formations

Members of the Special Operations Command Parachute Team perform their signature "stacking" maneuver, which allows them to land in sequence during an exhibition. Such performances generate interest in parachute operations.

in the sky. At 2,500 feet (760 m), members open their parachutes and join up in a maneuver known as "stacking," which allows them to land sequentially on the ground in formation, one behind the other. The team performs at military and civilian air shows, sporting events, and civic celebrations throughout the United States.

complete the course attend a graduation ceremony at Fort Benning. Completing formal schooling is not the end of training for Special Forces soldiers, however. Rangers train constantly in physical fitness and combat readiness exercises. Parachute jumps are practiced, generally monthly, to keep parachuting skills current, and intensive battle drills are conducted. Both rotary wing (helicopter) training with the 160th Special Operations Aviation Division and fixed wing (airplane) training are carried out frequently as well.

There are a variety of other specialized schools that Rangers can attend. These include Jumpmaster (parachuting teacher), Pathfinder (land navigation), Military Free Fall (falling before opening a parachute), and Ranger First Responder (rescue), among others.

AIRBORNE TRAINING

All soldiers involved in special operations and airborne missions must attend Airborne School at Fort Benning, Georgia. The Basic Airborne Course teaches soldiers how to parachute from planes and land safely. Training is divided into three weeks of increasingly rigorous training. During Ground Week, students undergo intensive training to learn how to correctly execute a parachute landing fall (PLF). To do so, a soldier must make five points of contact. These points collectively absorb the shock of landing by distributing the force of landing across the balls of the feet, calves, back of the thighs, buttocks, and shoulder muscles. They practice on mockups of aircraft to learn the proper way to exit a plane. During Tower Week, they apply the basics they have learned by performing jumps, starting with a 12-foot (3.6 m) platform and progressing to 250-foot (76 m) jumps. In the process, they must learn how to avoid obstacles and deal with parachute malfunctions.

The final week is Jump Week. Students perform real day and night jumps with various types of parachutes. They perform individual and mass jumps, including jumps while carrying equipment. Ultimately

Airborne operations students learn to parachute in simulated aircraft. Here, they prepare for a 34-foot (10 m) jump out the door of a mockup of a helicopter.

soldiers must make five successful jumps from a C-130 or C-17 aircraft at 1,250 feet (380 m).

AIR ASSAULT TRAINING

U.S. Army Air Assault School is a ten-day course designed to prepare soldiers for missions from helicopters, including insertion and evacuation. Just being accepted to Air Assault School is demanding. Before being accepted as a student, applicants must

Students in Air Assault School practice rappelling techniques, using ropes to climb into and out of helicopters. They also learn fast rope techniques to exit the aircraft in hostile situations.

complete a 12-mile (19 km) march and an obstacle course. On the day before formal training starts, students must successfully complete a 2-mile (3.2 km) run and another obstacle course. On the next day, students perform a 6-mile (9.7 km) march and undergo a thorough inspection. The first phase of training is the Combat Assault Phase. Over a three-day period, soldiers learn about aircraft safety and orientation, performing medical evacuation, land navigation (pathfinder) techniques, and combat assault operations. At the end of this period, they must pass a practical and written test.

The second phase is Slingload Operations. Students learn to load equipment weighing from 1,000 to 8,000 pounds (450 to 3,630 kilograms) on a helicopter, using a sling tethered to the underbelly of the helicopter. Again, students must pass a hands-on and written test. The third phase is the Rappelling Phase. This means they must use a rope to climb down a steep incline. Air assault soldiers must be able to rappel from aircraft. To complete this phase, soldiers must be able to rappel from a 34-foot (10 m) tower and perform two rappels of 70 to 90 feet (21 to 27 m) from a hovering Black Hawk helicopter. Finally, soldiers reach graduation day. Their final task is to complete a 12-mile (19 km) march with full gear and rucksack in under three hours.

AVIATION TRAINING

Airborne and air assault operations rely on expert helicopter pilots. To become a helicopter pilot, one must attend Aviation School. To attend, one must be an officer or warrant officer (someone assigned officer status because of a special technical skill). Students at Aviation School begin by learning basic flying skills. This requires hours of classroom as well as practical study. Students must learn the physics of flight, flight systems, map reading and drawing, emergency procedures, and many more subjects. Students then move on to hands-on training in helicopter flying, including combat maneuvers. Students then get specialized training in one of the various types of helicopters used by the army. Among these are the OH-58 Kiowa, UH-60 Black Hawk, AH-64 Apache, and CH-47 Chinook.

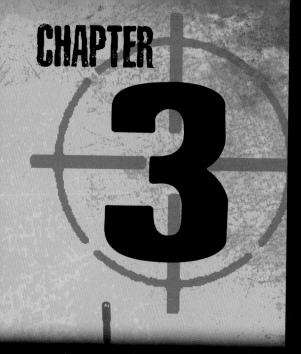

OPERATION JUST CAUSE

O peration Just Cause, the U.S. invasion of Panama, provides an excellent example of large-scale twentieth-century special operations. It was an extremely complex mission that relied on striking nearly two dozen targets within twenty-four hours. Operation Just Cause typifies the modern U.S. approach to military operations, which rely on speed and precision, and aim to minimize damage to civilians. Airborne units played a key role in the action. This was a major special ops mission for the 160th SOAR(A), 75th Rangers (Airborne), 82nd Airborne, and 101st Air

U.S. troops patrol an area near the Panamanian Defense headquarters in Panama City during Operation Just Cause in December 1989. A variety of special operations teams were involved in the action.

GEAR

Everything air commandos use must be able to be carried during a drop from an aircraft. Therefore, it is important that equipment be lightweight and compact. The basic pack used today is the All-purpose Lightweight Individual Carrying Equipment (ALICE). It is an aluminum frame to which is attached a large pack and cargo shelf and which is worn with shoulder straps. In airborne operations, it is attached by a tether to the paratrooper and held between his legs until his chute opens. Once the chute opens, the ALICE is allowed to hang down to make it easier for the paratrooper to land.

In a firefight, a long trek, or some special missions, the ALICE is too heavy and bulky. In these situations the soldiers wear load bearing gear (LC-2). This gear consists of a belt supported by suspender-like straps. Various pouches and containers can be attached to the belt. Typically a Special Forces soldier will carry on his body ammunition, weapons, food, water, explosives, a first-aid kit, and any special gear necessary for a three- to five-day mission. The military has also started using vests to which various types of pouches can be attached as an alternative to the LC-2.

Weapons, too, must be lightweight and portable. For this reason, air commando units use weapons like the M4 carbine, a small, compact version of the full-size M16 carbine rifle. Different types of add-ons

(continued on the next page)

(continued from the previous page)

can be added to the M4, making it a modular combat system. Add-ons include low-light and thermal imaging systems, which allow soldiers to see in darkness or where there is little light; laser sights for targeting; and a grenade launcher. Snipers, who are precision shooters, carry the M24 sniper rifle. As with rifles, air commandos use lightweight versions of machine guns. Among these is the M249 Squad Automatic Weapon (SAW). They also carry M9 Beretta pistols and a survival knife. Pilots carry a separate tool, called a strapcutter multitool. It has a J-hook that can be used for cutting seatbelts and straps to free air crew in downed planes. For protection, the soldiers wear Kevlar helmets and body armor.

Assault. Although many different types of military units were involved in this operation, many major objectives relied heavily on the use of airborne Special Forces, several of which are highlighted here.

PROVOCATION

On the night of December 16, 1989, four off-duty U.S. military officers driving in a civilian automobile through Panama City, Panama, were stopped by guards at a Panama Defense Forces (PDF) roadblock and ordered out of their car. Fearing the mob that was gathering around them, the officers refused and began to drive off. The guards opened fire and fatally wounded one of the officers. The PDF guards seized a navy lieutenant and his wife, who had witnessed the event. They were taken to PDF headquarters in Panama City, where the lieutenant was interrogated and beaten before being released hours later.

In response to the incident and the danger to Americans in Panama, President George H. W. Bush authorized military intervention in Panama. In a speech explaining his decision to invade Panama, Bush stated that the purpose of the intervention was to "safeguard the lives of Americans, to defend democracy in Panama, to combat drug trafficking, and to protect the integrity of the Panama Canal Treaty." President Bush subsequently ordered the military to apprehend Manuel Noriega, the country's military dictator. The operation to invade Panama was dubbed Operation Just Cause and was implemented under the direction of General Maxwell Thurman.

INVASION

According to the U.S. Army publication on the invasion, *Operation Just Cause: The Invasion of Panama*, on December 19, 1989, at Fort Bragg in North Carolina, air commados began going through the preparation for deployment: restriction to unit areas, issuance of firearms, and packing of equipment. A task force of the First Brigade of the 82nd Airborne Division, consisting of twenty aircraft, arrived at nearby Pope Air Force Base in freezing rain. The icy rain became more serious as night fell, but the commanders made the decision to get as many aircraft airborne as possible.

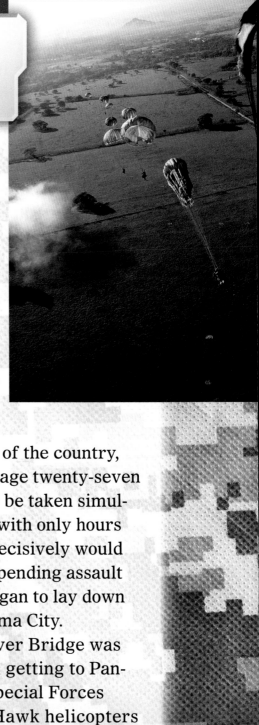

U.S. airborne special operations soldiers parachute into an area near Panama City, Panama, during Operation Just Cause, prepared to seize or control twenty-seven different targets.

At the time of the invasion, the United States had thirteen thousand troops stationed in Panama. Airlifts brought in a strike force of approximately seven thousand troops. The troops included a joint brigade consisting of the 82nd Airborne Division, the 75th Rangers, and five battalions' worth of other Special Forces. These were subsequently supplemented by another seven thousand soldiers. To defeat Noriega's military forces and take control of the country, these soldiers needed to seize or engage twenty-seven different targets. About half were to be taken simultaneously. The rest were to be dealt with only hours after the first. Striking swiftly and decisively would minimize casualties. News of the impending assault leaked out, however, and the PDF began to lay down roadblocks and move troops to Panama City.

Gaining control of the Pacora River Bridge was the key to keeping PDF forces from getting to Panama City. Just before 1:00 AM, the Special Forces attack began. Three UH-60 Black Hawk helicopters

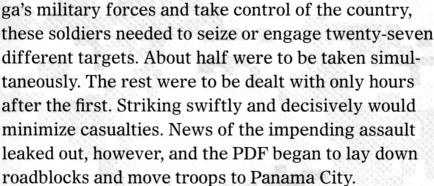

delivered the Special Forces to the bridge as the PDF forces were approaching. An AC-130 gunship was called in, and it pinned down the PDF forces with fire from the air. The air commandos were able to maintain control of the bridge, blocking the PDF from entering Panama City or reaching Omar Torrijos International Airport and Tocumen Military Airfield—major objectives of the U.S. attack.

Capturing these two adjacent airports would accomplish two important goals. It would allow the U.S. forces to neutralize the 2nd PDF Company and the Panamanian air force located there, and it would make it impossible for Noriega to use one of the airports to escape capture. Two AH-6 attack helicopters and one AC-130 gunship attacked specific targets around Tocumen Airfield, keeping them pinned down until four companies of Rangers could parachute in from 500 feet (150 m). The Rangers quickly secured the airports in time for the paratroopers from the 82nd Airborne to begin dropping in around 2:00 AM.

LA COMANDANCIA

Attack helicopters from the 160th Special Operations Aviation Group began an assault on the PDF headquarters, La Comandancia, at forty-five minutes after midnight. According to the U.S. Army booklet *Operation Just Cause*,

The lead helicopter, an AH-6 "Light Bird," was shot down and crashed into the courtyard

This photo shows the bombed-out shell of the Panamanian Defense headquarters building in Panama City on December 27, 1989, in the wake of Operation Just Cause.

of the *PDF* headquarters. The two-man crew was not injured and successfully evaded both hostile and friendly fire. The men escaped from the compound, armed only with pistols, and captured a *PDF* soldier, scaled the outer wall, and linked up with the mechanized company just as it arrived on the scene.

The battle around the PDF headquarters became so intense that it was nearly impossible to see through the smoke and fire generated by the continuous firing from the helicopters and explosions. Eventually, a Ranger company from Torrijos Airport arrived. The Rangers cleared the remaining PDF in the headquarters building and secured them, achieving another objective.

THE CAPTURE OF NORIEGA

Noriega was in the area when the parachute assault began. He fled instantly. His two-car motorcade was stopped at a roadblock, but Noriega's car managed to evade capture. There was concern that he might try to leave the country from the military airfield near his beach house, located about 50 miles (80.5 km) from the Panama Canal zone. Two F-117A stealth aircraft each dropped a bomb on the military base. As soon as the bombs hit, an AC-130 gunship and Black Hawk helicopters joined the fray. Five minutes later, the air was filled with paratroopers. When the sun came up, the base was secure.

Within days, all of Noriega's military forces had been subdued and the military targets were secured. However, Manuel Noriega hadn't been captured, and his whereabouts were unknown. Sightings of Noriega made it clear that he had not left the country, but despite forty actions to find him, he couldn't be tracked down. The military was concerned that he might seek refuge at the embassy of another country. However, where he sought refuge was the last place they expected to find someone with his past association with drugs and crime.

On the afternoon of December 24, he had taken refuge in the Vatican Embassy with the aid of the papal nuncio (a diplomatic representative of the pope). As soon as Noriega's location was identified, negotiations began between the state department and the Vatican. When word leaked out that Noriega was in the embassy, a crowd gathered, chanting anti-Noriega slogans. Military personnel were pressed into service for crowd control. Finally, on January 3, 1990, Noriega gave up and left the embassy. He was taken into custody by U.S. authorities, flown to Miami, and charged with drug trafficking. Two years after the invasion, he was convicted of racketeering, drug trafficking, and money laundering. He was sentenced to forty years in prison.

After combat ended, U.S. soldiers turned to cleanup tasks. They patrolled the streets to keep order and collected remaining caches of arms and members of the PDF, often turned in by Panamanian citizens who had suffered under Noriega's rule. They also assisted civilians with cleanup and recovery.

AIR COMMANDOS IN AFGHANISTAN AND IRAQ

The 160th Special Operations Aviation Regiment (Airborne) (SOAR)(A) played a key role in a number of special operations in both Afghanistan and Iraq. This chapter covers two high-profile actions by SOAR(A).

THE BATTLE OF TAKUR GHAR, 2002

Special operations were carried out by the 160th SOAR(A) in March 2002 as part of the battle of Takur Ghar, a 10,000-foot (3,000 m) mountain in Afghanistan. The battle was part of Operation Anaconda, whose goal was to destroy Al Qaeda forces in the area. Operation Anaconda involved members of the 101st Airborne and Special Forces units including members of the 75th Ranger Regiment, Navy SEALs, and Air Force Special Operations Command, as well as Coalition and Northern Alliance troops.

Chinook helicopters were used to deliver paratroopers to eastern Afghanistan during Operation Anaconda in order to pursue Al Qaeda and Taliban forces in the area.

The operation's objective was to root out several hundred Al Qaeda and Taliban fighters south of Gardez in eastern Afghanistan. The U.S. forces were determined to establish an observation post on top of Takur Ghar, which afforded a view of the entire area. Al Qaeda was well aware of the desirability of the mountain outpost and set up an ambush for incoming U.S. forces. When the first 160th SOAR(A) helicopter approached, Al Qaeda operatives opened fire, hitting the craft with a rocket-propelled grenade (RPG). A Navy SEAL being transported on the craft, Petty Officer 1st Class Neil Roberts, fell from the helicopter. The damaged helicopter was forced to crash-land 7 miles (11 km) away. Another helicopter picked up the special operations team and delivered it back to Roberts's last known location. The team attempted to rescue Roberts but was forced to break off contact when the firefight with the enemy became too intense.

The quick-reaction force of the 75th Ranger Regiment was called in to effect the rescue. The twenty-three-man team boarded other 160th SOAR(A) helicopters and headed back to Takur Ghar. One helicopter was shot down at the top of the mountain. A second deposited the rest of the Rangers at another site, and they climbed 2,000 feet (610 m) and joined up with the other Special Forces team. The Rangers closed in on the Al Qaeda forces and destroyed them. They then had to wait till night for extraction. Seven members of the Special Forces were killed in the course of the mission. Around 8:15 PM, four helicopters from the 160th SOAR(A) extracted the Rangers as well as the SEALs who were farther down the mountain. Two hours later, the wounded were met by the 274th Forward Surgical Team, who were located at the Bagram Airport tower. In the morning, the wounded were taken to hospitals in Europe. Operation Anaconda went on for another nineteen days, and the same units played a key role in defeating other enemy forces.

MISSION AT AL QADISIYAH, 2003

During the early stages of Operation Iraqi Freedom (2003–2010), the 160th SOAR(A) airlifted a joint task force of Special Forces units, including Delta Force and Ranger units, into the field. The objective was an assault on the compound at Al Qadisiyah, a desert town in Iraq that was suspected of containing chemical weapons. The mission used ten transportation MH-6 Little Birds, UH-60 Black Hawks, and MH-47 Chinooks, and four Little Bird and Black Hawk gunships.

The mission began at approximately midnight on March 23, 2003, with a sweep of the ground from helicopters to ascertain if there were any Iraqi troops in the area. Two gunships armed with miniguns and rocket pods followed. Next came helicopters that delivered the Rangers, who established themselves around the area as a guard force. Gunfire erupted from surrounding buildings. A gunship armed with rockets and a helicopter carrying airborne snipers began to suppress enemy fire. The special operations forces began to go through the complex, searching the labs, offices, and storage areas for evidence of weapons of mass destruction (WMD). Information on what they found has not been released.

From the sky the gunships swept the ground, searching for enemy forces, while the Rangers exchanged fire with the enemy. When the special operations forces completed their search, they reboarded the Chinook helicopters. Once they were safely away, the Rangers boarded the Black Hawks and left the area guarded by the gunships of the 160th.

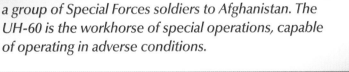

A UH-60 Blackhawk helicopter takes off after delivering a group of Special Forces soldiers to Afghanistan. The UH-60 is the workhorse of special operations, capable of operating in adverse conditions.

THE DEATH OF OSAMA BIN LADEN

Osama bin Laden was the founder and leader of the terrorist group Al Qaeda. On May 2, 2011, he was killed in Pakistan by a raid carried out by U.S. Special Forces, including Navy SEAL Team Six and the 160th SOAR(A). The operation was codenamed Operation Neptune Spear.

The CIA spearheaded the effort to locate bin Laden. Bin Laden was known to avoid electronic

HELICOPTERS

Air commandos rely on helicopters for transportation and protection. Several different types of helicopters are used by airborne Special Forces:

UH-60 Black Hawk: The Black Hawk is the army's all-around helicopter. Powerful and maneuverable, it is used for both assault and transportation. It is also used for medical missions. It carries a crew of four and can transport a fully equipped twelve-man Special Forces team. It is used for clandestine penetration of enemy territory, for reconnaissance, and for the insertion and extraction of Special Forces teams. It can work in the dark and in adverse weather conditions.

MH-60L Direct-Action Penetrator (DAP): The MH-60L DAP is a variant of the Black Hawk helicopter designed to function as a gunship. Its main mission is to provide armed escort and fire support for Special Forces missions, in particular during the insertion and extraction of small units of Special Forces. It is mounted with miniguns, chain guns, and rocket launchers and air-to-air missiles.

MH-47 Chinook: The Chinook is built for heavy lifting and is used to move a large number of soldiers or large amounts of ammunition or supplies. It is a twin-turbine, tandem rotor helicopter. It is equipped with weather avoidance/search radar, secure communications, and a fast-rope insertion/extraction system. A fast-rope system allows ropes to be secured on the outside of the helicopter so that soldiers can slide down them, allowing for very fast insertion. The MH-47 is capable of operating at night as well as day. It can be reconfigured with special equipment for a variety of types of missions.

Little Bird: The MH-6M mission-enhanced Little Bird is a single-engine light utility helicopter. It is used for short-range insertion/extraction operations. It is also used to resupply soldiers and for assault missions in hostile territory. In addition, it is employed in rescue and recovery operations. Being small, it can operate from ships and platforms and in urban terrain. It has fast-rope systems on both sides and can also be rigged with a caving ladder for insertion/extraction in tight locations.

OH-58 Kiowa Warrior: The Kiowa Warrior is rapidly deployable. Two can be transported by a C-130 aircraft because the main rotor blades and other external components fold away. They are used for light defensive, reconnaissance, target identification, and other combat support applications.

AH-64 Apache Longbow: The AH-64 Apache is a heavy attack helicopter. It incorporates advanced radar, missiles, and control systems. It can undertake close and deep precision strikes. It is also used for reconnaissance at night, over obscured battlefields, and in adverse weather conditions.

AH-6J Light Attack Helicopter (LAH): The AH-6J LAH is a single-turbine-engine light attack helicopter. It is usually flown by two pilots. It is most often used for close air support of soldiers on the ground. It is also used in target destruction raids and to escort and protect transportation or supply helicopters.

communication, which he worried would be tapped into and reveal his location. To communicate with his Al Qaeda associates, he used a messenger. Eventually, the CIA identified the messenger and used this knowledge to locate a three-story compound at the end of a dirt road northeast of the center of Abbottabad as the place bin Laden was hiding. The building was surrounded by a concrete wall with barbed wire on top and had two security gates. The compound had no telephone or Internet service, and instead of putting out their trash for pickup like their neighbors, the inhabitants burned it.

The 160th SOAR used two Black Hawk helicopters to fly in two teams of Navy SEALs. The raid was launched from northeastern Afghanistan. The helicopters were stealth versions, which fly more quietly and are more difficult for radar to detect than regular Black Hawks. Additional SOAR Chinook helicopters were stationed at the Afghan border in case backup was needed.

There was little moonlight that night, and the helicopters entered Pakistan keeping low to the ground to avoid detection. As they approached the compound, one helicopter grazed a wall and was forced to make a soft crash landing. It was later destroyed to keep its technology from falling into the wrong hands. The other helicopter landed near the exterior of the compound. The SEALs from both helicopters scaled the compound's walls. The compound was completely dark because the CIA had cut the power to the neighborhood. Once inside, the SEALs found

One helicopter crashed near a wall during the Special Forces' attack on Osama bin Laden's compound in Abbottabad, Pakistan, during which bin Laden was killed.

inhabitants in the guest house, the first floor of the main house, and finally in the last part of the compound to be searched—the second and third floors where bin Laden and his family lived.

Bin Laden's courier, Abu Ahmed al-Kuwaiti, fired on the SEALs from behind the guesthouse door and was killed in the ensuing firefight. Al-Kuwaiti's brother Abrar and his wife were shot on the first floor of the main house. Bin Laden's adult son rushed the SEALs on the staircase and was killed. Bin Laden looked down from the third floor at the advancing SEALs and retreated into his room. The SEALs followed, shooting bin Laden. (Bin Laden's body was taken back to the United States.) The other residents were left at the compound and eventually arrested by the Pakistanis. From the team's arrival to departure, the raid took thirty-eight minutes.

CHAPTER 5

FIGHTING TERRORISTS AND DEALING WITH DISASTER

The current mission of the 82nd Airborne is primarily counterinsurgency, responding to hotbeds of political upheaval. This section discusses some of the missions of the 82nd Airborne to root out terrorists in the Middle East. The 82nd Airborne has played a major role in recent natural disasters as well. One of the first units on the scene in recent disasters, it has played an important part in natural disasters such as Hurricane Katrina and the 2010 earthquake in Haiti.

OPERATION CLEAN SWEEP

In Afghanistan and Iraq, the 82nd Airborne has played an important role in working with local forces to hunt down the Taliban, Al Qaeda, and other criminal elements, as well as locate weapons. Operation Clean Sweep illustrates how they approach this type of mission.

These paratroopers from the 82nd Airborne patrol an area. The purpose of patrols such as these is to search for suspicious activity or articles that might mean insurgents or terrorists are in the area.

In February 2007, the crew of aircraft observing an area in Tikrit, Iraq, reported the suspicious presence of a large number of empty ammunition boxes in the area, leading them to wonder if there was an insurgent cell with a cache of weapons in the area. Air commandos from the 82nd Airborne and soldiers from the Iraqi army embarked on a mission to locate and destroy the insurgent training site, supported by helicopters from various aviation divisions. The paratroopers were accompanied by Eddie, a bomb-sniffing dog.

When the paratroopers reached the ground from UH-60 Black Hawk helicopters, they immediately set up a defensive perimeter. They then proceeded

QUICK-STRIKE FORCE

In 2012, President Barack Obama ordered the reactivation of the 82nd Airborne's Ready Brigade, a quick-strike force, to land powerful military forces swiftly anywhere in the world. A quick-strike force is designed to be ready to deploy within hours of an alert. Its role is to intervene to gain and hold ground in quickly unfolding combat or in situations such as uprisings that require the immediate evacuation of foreign embassies.

Having quick-strike forces gives the president the ability to land powerful military forces anywhere in the world within a very short amount of time. The objectives of the 82nd Airborne quick-strike force could include evacuating American citizens, safeguarding fragile new democracies from counterattack, and taking down a renegade regime, among others.

For the past ten years, the 82nd Airborne has undertaken missions in small units, either squads of nine to twelve soldiers or platoons with thirty to forty soldiers, often working with local soldiers and villagers. The Ready Brigade works with larger numbers of soldiers — up to hundreds — that can be airlifted with a few hours' notice. Establishing the quick-strike force expands the role of the 82nd Airborne from a narrow focus on counterinsurgency to a wider variety of missions requiring rapid response.

to search the buildings in the area. In a cluster of brick and mud buildings near the airfield, they discovered what appeared to be an insurgent training site. It contained rocket-propelled grenade launchers, mortars, blank ammunition for use in training, and training diagrams. Eddie proceeded to explore the area, sniffing out ammunition and explosives as his trainer followed, rewarding him for his finds with dog treats.

Once all the ammunition and weapons were collected, the soldiers photographed the cache. Ordnance specialists then placed explosive charges. The charges went off, destroying the weapons and the buildings that had housed them.

HURRICANE KATRINA

Hurricane Katrina, which struck the Gulf Coast of the United States in 2005, was one of the five deadliest hurricanes in the history of the United States. At least 1,833 people died in the hurricane and subsequent floods. When it struck New Orleans, levees constructed to hold back water from Lake Ponchartrain collapsed, and water from the lake added to the flooding in the city. In some places the water was up to the roofs of houses. Thousands of people were stranded without resources. A vast number of those who fled their flooded dwellings took refuge in the New Orleans Convention Center and the Super Dome. Major General William Caldwell of the 82nd Airborne received succinct orders from Lieutenant General Honore, commander of Joint Task Force Katrina, who was responsible for coordinating military relief efforts for Hurricane Katrina: "Your job is to fix the airport and fix New Orleans."

Only seven hours after receiving their orders, units from the 82nd Airborne began arriving at the New Orleans Airport. Evacuating people was a critical need. Working with airport staff, the 319th Airborne Field Artillery took over passenger manifests and security screening. Within twelve hours, they had evacuated nine thousand people via the airport.

Search and rescue was another issue. The 3rd Brigade of the 82nd Airborne worked on search and rescue operations. They provided the Federal Emergency Management Agency (FEMA) with manpower, equipment, and maps. Soldiers from the 82nd Airborne evacuated the Super Dome and the Convention Center, seeing that people got safely to other locations. In addition, to ensure safety in the city, the paratroopers joined National Guard units in patrolling the streets.

HAITIAN EARTHQUAKE

On January 12, 2010, the island country of Haiti experienced a 7.0 magnitude earthquake. The epicenter of the massive earthquake was near Léogâne, about 16 miles (25 km) west of the capital city of Port-au-Prince. According to the U.S. Geological Survey, the initial shock was followed by at least thirty-three aftershocks, fourteen of which were between magnitudes 5.0 and 5.9. International Red Cross estimates were that the earthquake affected around three million people. The

Haitian government reported that more than 316,000 were killed and estimated that 300,000 were injured and about one million were homeless.

Within days, fifty members of the 2nd Brigade (2nd BCT) of the U.S. 82nd Airborne Division started arriving in crippled Port-au-Prince. Hundreds more soldiers would follow. The global response force, the 2nd BCT is on 24/7 standby. It is ready to deploy anywhere in the world within eighteen hours. Relief efforts began with the distribution of food and water to several hundred Haitians from makeshift tents on a soccer field. Throngs of hungry Haitians pushed forward, rushing the military trucks.

In addition to humanitarian relief, the 82nd Airborne provided security.

In one example, eight Jordanian U.N. troops had set up a World Health Organization–run warehouse containing some eighty tons of medical supplies. One of the walls of the warehouse had collapsed during the earthquake. The 2nd BCT joined the Jordanians at the

Members of the 82nd Airborne deliver supplies of food to a refugee camp in Port-au-Prince, Haiti, after the 2010 earthquake. They also treated the wounded and cleared debris, among other activities.

warehouse to provide security to protect the supplies from looters. They set up camp in an open steel-framed pavilion without running water or electrical generators. Many of the soldiers had to sleep on the ground.

The 82nd Airborne set up a refugee camp on a Port-au-Prince golf course, eventually housing fifty thousand displaced Haitians. At the camp, the soldiers distributed thousands of meals and bottles of water each day and ran a medical clinic. While they administered the camp, the soldiers slept on adjacent tennis courts.

THE FUTURE OF AIRBORNE SPECIAL OPS

Special operations have become a key element in both military and national security missions. One of the most important responsibilities of the military will be to identify, locate, and stop terrorists. In the foreseeable future, the role of the military will most likely continue to shift from large-scale military battles to actions that require small, more flexible units. As part of this approach, the role of airborne special operations teams is likely to continue to expand.

Over the next decade, it is likely that the military will develop increasingly advanced stealth helicopters and more advanced unmanned drone aircraft. These aircraft will be equipped with more sensitive information-gathering technology and communications systems. Airborne Special Forces will continue to carry out independent missions. However, because of the global nature of terrorist

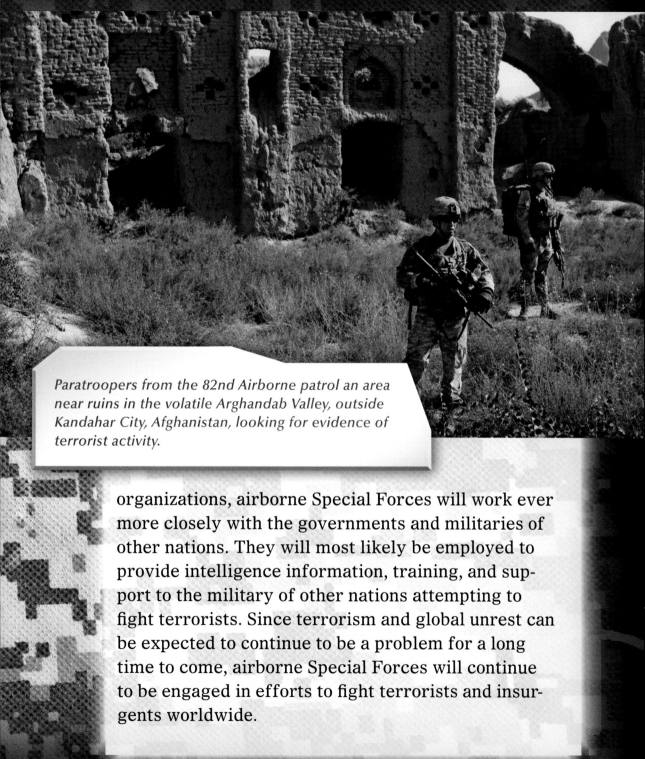

Paratroopers from the 82nd Airborne patrol an area near ruins in the volatile Arghandab Valley, outside Kandahar City, Afghanistan, looking for evidence of terrorist activity.

organizations, airborne Special Forces will work ever more closely with the governments and militaries of other nations. They will most likely be employed to provide intelligence information, training, and support to the military of other nations attempting to fight terrorists. Since terrorism and global unrest can be expected to continue to be a problem for a long time to come, airborne Special Forces will continue to be engaged in efforts to fight terrorists and insurgents worldwide.

GLOSSARY

CACHE Items, such as weapons, that are hidden or stored away.

CLANDESTINE Secret.

COUNTERINSURGENCY Actions taken against those engaging in guerrilla warfare or attempting to bring down a government.

CREED An organization's statement of values.

DEPLOY Embark on a military operation.

GUERRILLA WARFARE Unexpected attacks carried out by unofficial forces.

INSURGENT A revolutionary.

INTERVENTION Becoming involved in the affairs of another country.

LIGHT INFANTRY Soldiers who carry only compact and portable weapons and equipment so they can move swiftly and flexibly.

MEDEVAC/CASEVAC Medical evacuation and casualty evaluation; the removal of the injured from the area where a battle has taken place so they can receive medical treatment.

ORDNANCE Weapons and ammunition.

RECONNAISSANCE To scout out the features of an area, the location and movements of troops and weapons, and other valuable information.

UNCONVENTIONAL WARFARE Military actions conducted from inside enemy lines using specialized techniques.

FOR MORE INFORMATION

Airborne and Special Forces Museum
100 Bragg Boulevard
Fayetteville, NC 28301
(910) 643-2766
Website: http://www.asomf.org
   The exhibits at this museum begin in 1940 and continue to today's special operations and airborne forces.

The Armed Forces History Museum
2050 34th Way North
Largo, FL 33771
(727) 539-8371
Website: http://armedforcesmuseum.com
   This museum contains exhibits exploring military endeavors and wars throughout America's history.

Canadian Military Heritage Museum
347 Greenwich Street
Brantford, ON N3S 7X4
Canada
(519) 759-1313
Website: http://www.cmhmhq.ca
   This museum features exhibits of artifacts pertaining to Canada's military history.

Canadian War Museum
1 Vimy Place

Ottawa, ON K1A 0M8
Canada
(819) 776-7000
(800) 555-5621
Website: http://www.warmuseum.ca
> The Canadian War Museum tells the story of Canada's military history and how it affected the development of Canada.

Fort Benning Maneuver Center of Excellence

Public Affairs Office
1 Karker Street, McGinnis-Wickam Hall, Suite W-141
Fort Benning, GA 31905
(706) 545-2236
Website: http://www.benning.army.mil
> The Maneuver Center of Excellence provides information on the various training programs for Special Forces soldiers.

John F. Kennedy Special Warfare Museum

Fort Bragg
Ardennes Road
Fort Bragg, NC 28310
(910) 432-1533
Website: http://www.soc.mil/swcs/museum.html
> This museum features exhibits on the history of the Special Forces, civil affairs, and psychological operations units.

Special Operations Warrior Foundation

1137 Marbella Plaza Drive

Tampa, FL 33619

(813) 805-9400

(813) 805-0640

Website: http://www.specialops.org/?page=Contact_Us

   This foundation provides scholarships and educational and family counseling to the children of special operations personnel who have died in the line of duty and financial grants to wounded special operations personnel.

U.S. Special Operations Command

Headquarters, United States Special Operations
   Command

7701 Tampa Point Boulevard

MacDill Air Force Base, FL 33621

(813) 826-4600

Website: http://www.socom.mil/Pages/
   AboutUSSOCOM.aspx

   The U.S. Special Operations Command oversees various branches of the Special Forces and maintains the Special Operations Command Parachute Team.

WEBSITES

Because of the changing nature of Internet links, Rosen Publishing has developed an online list of websites related to the subject of this book. This site is updated regularly. Please use this link to access this list:

http://www.rosenlinks.com/ISF/AirCo

FOR FURTHER READING

Earl, C. F. *Green Berets*. Broomall, PA: Mason Crest Publishing, 2010.

Gregory, Josh. *Cool Military Careers: Special Ops*. North Mankato, MN: Cherry Lake Publishing, 2012.

Montana, Jack. *Elite Forces Selection*. Broomall, PA: Mason Crest Publishing, 2010.

Montana, Jack. *Parachute Regiment*. Broomall, PA: Mason Crest Publishing, 2010.

Nardo, Don. *Special Operations: Paratroopers*. Greensboro, NC: Morgan Reynolds, 2012.

Nardo, Don. *Special Operations: Search and Rescue*. Greensboro, NC: Morgan Reynolds, 2013.

Nardo, Don. *Special Operations: Training*. Greensboro, NC: Morgan Reynolds, 2012.

Ryan, Peter. *Black Ops and Other Special Missions of the U.S. Air Force Combat Control Team*. New York, NY: Rosen Publishing, 2012.

Stephenson, Mark, Jay Davos, and Suzie Snyder. *Tactical Strength and Conditioning: Training for the Tactical Athlete—Special Forces Selection and Assessment*. Colorado Springs, CO: National Strength and Conditioning Association, 2007.

Sutherland, Donald. *Special Forces: The Thrill, the Missions, the Danger*. Minneapolis, MN: Lerner Publishing Group, 2012.

Vanderhoof, Gabrielle, and C. F. Earl. *Army Rangers*. Broomall, PA: Mason Crest Publishers, 2010.

BIBLIOGRAPHY

American Special Ops. "Mission at Al Qadisiyah."
   Retrieved February 3, 2014 (http://www
   .americanspecialops.com/night-stalkers/
   operations/wmd-site-iraq).

Bracken, Amy. "At Haitian Golf Course, 82nd Air-
   borne Runs a Refugee Camp." *Christian Science
   Monitor*, January 21, 2010. Retrieved February
   2014 (http://www.csmonitor.com/World/
   Americas/2010/0121/At-Haiti-golf-course-82nd
   -Airborne-runs-a-refugee-camp).

Bryant, Susan, and Russ Bryant. *Screaming Eagles:
   101st Airborne Division*. Minneapolis, MN: Zenith
   Press, 2007.

Cohen, Scott. "Operation Nowruz Jhala." *America's
   North Shore Journal*. Retrieved February 4,
   2014 (http://northshorejournal.org/operation
   -nowruz-jhala).

Durant, Michael J. *The Night Stalkers: Top
   Secret Missions of the U.S.'s Special
   Operations Aviation Regiment*. New York, NY:
   Penguin, 2008.

Entous, Adam. "U.S. 82nd's 'Beast' Helps Hungry
   Haitians." Reuters, January 22, 2010. Retrieved
   February 7, 2014 (http://www.reuters.com/
   article/2010/01/22/us-quake-haiti-airborne
   -idUSTRE60L3CA20100122).

Fort Bragg. "82nd Airborne Division." Retrieved January 20, 2014 (http://www.bragg.army.mil/82nd/Pages/History.aspx).

Garamone, Jim. "The Battle of Takur Gar." Armed Forces News Service/U.S. Department of Defense. Retrieved February 4, 2014 (http://www.defense.gov/news/newsarticle.aspx?id=44020).

Pushies, Fred. *82nd Airborne*. Minneapolis, MN: Zenith Press, 2008.

Sarasota Herald Tribune. "Stepping Out into the Blue." Retrieved February 1, 2014 (http://news.google.com/newspapers?nid=1755&dat=20050318&id=LXAfAAAAIBAJ&sjid=HIUEAAAAIBAJ&pg=4105,4636835).

SOFREF. "Rangers: A Day in the Life—A Day in the Life of an Army Ranger." Retrieved February 2, 2014 (http://sofrep.com/army-rangers/a-day-in-the-life).

U.S. Army. "The Army Response to Hurricane Katrina." Retrieved February 6, 2014 (http://www.army.mil/article/45029/The_Army_response_to_Hurricane_Katrina).

U.S. Army. "106 Special Operations Aviation Regiment." Retrieved January 20, 2014 (http://www.soc.mil/ARSOAC/160th.html).

U.S. Army. "Rangers: History and Heritage." Retrieved January 20, 2014 (http://www.army.mil/ranger/heritage.html).

U.S. Army. "Special Forces: Training." Retrieved January 21, 2014 (http://www.goarmy.com/special-forces/training.html).

U.S. Army Maneuver Center of Excellence. "Airborne and Ranger Training Brigade." Retrieved February 5, 2014 (http://www.benning.army.mil/infantry/rtb).

U.S. Army Special Operations Command. "160th Special Operations Aviation Regiment." Retrieved January 4, 2014 (http://www.soc.mil/ARSOAC/160th.html).

U.S. Department of Defense. "Executive Summary of the Battle of Takur Gar." May 24, 2002. Retrieved February 4, 2014 (http://www.defense.gov/news/May2002/d20020524takurghar.pdf).

INDEX

ABOUT THE AUTHOR

Jeri Freedman has a B.A. from Harvard University. She is the author of more than thirty-five young adult nonfiction books, many published by Rosen Publishing, including *Careers in Emergency Medical Response Teams' Search and Rescue*, *America Debates: Civil Liberties and Terrorism*, and *The Call of Duty: Your Career in the Air Force*.

PHOTO CREDITS

Cover inset photos www.army.mil, from left U.S. Air Force Tech. Sgt. Manuel J. Martinez, Capt. Rebecca Walsh, NTC Operations, Sgt. 1st Class Christopher DeHart, 36th Infantry Division USD-S Public Affairs; cover background (flare) © iStockphoto.com/Evgeny Terentev; cover background (smoke) © iStockphoto.com/Antagain; cover background and interior (crosshairs) © iStockphoto.com/marlanu; p. 5 Dieter Spears/Vetta/Getty Images; p. 9 Yuri Cortez/AFP/Getty Images; p. 11 Co Rentmeester/The Life Picture Collection/Getty Images; p. 16 SuperStock/Getty Images; p. 20 Bob Rosato/Sports Illustrated/Getty Images; p. 23 USSOCOM photo; p. 25 U.S. Army photo/Mrs. Cheryl Rodewig; p. 26 U.S. Army photo/Sgt. Ken Scar; p. 28 Manoocher Deghati/AFP/Getty Images; p. 32 © Everett Collection Historical/Alamy; pp. 34, 47, 51, 53 © AP Images; p. 38 Joe Raedle/Getty Images; p. 41 Jonathan Saruk/Getty Images; p. 45 AFP/Getty Images; interior graphics © iStockphoto.com/P_Wei (camouflage), © iStockphoto.com/Oleg Zabielin (silhouette), © iStockphoto.com/gary milner (texture).

Designer: Brian Garvey; Editor: Christine Poolos